My Guide to Medicare

HEALTH CARE COSTS ARE THE LARGEST UNKNOWN EXPENSE FOR OLDER AMERICANS

E. Denise Panczykowski

Denise Panczykowski
Medicare Consulting, Inc. Publishing
P.O. Box 955
Ponte Vedra Beach, FL 32004

denise@medicare-consultant.com
www.medicare-consultant.com

DEDICATION

This book is dedicated to my clients and friends. You have taught me so much about how Americans are struggling to meet the ever-increasing *costs* of health care. And, while trying to manage your own *health* issues, you are often caring for family members.

I admire your strength in caring for aging parents, a sibling, adult children, and even grandchildren! We are *all* facing the same challenges! Talk about stress! *And, we thought after working for so many years, we would be sitting on the beach, watching the sunset, and sipping an adult beverage!!!*

This scenario is a constant reminder to me that we need to take charge of our own health, and return to preventive and holistic care of ourselves, as much as possible. We <u>can</u> *choose* to impact our own health.

ACKNOWLEDGMENTS

Special thanks to my friends, co-workers, Sherri C., and clients, who have encouraged me to pursue my passion – learning and teaching, and learning. They go hand in hand.

In this instance, I hope this book allows you to become very "learned" on the subject of Medicare. Be confident and comfortable, in making the important decisions you have coming up!

CONTENT

INTRODUCTION

Congratulations! You are about to seize the opportunity to *quickly* and *easily* learn about Medicare.

My goal is to make this "education" *less confusing*, less stressful and less time consuming, and I dare say, "easy"! I am confident this guide will help you succeed at those tasks!

I have *intentionally* kept this book very brief. The official government Medicare Guide is 136 pages, as of the time of writing this book. Other people have written Medicare guides with over 300 pages. Do you *really* want to read volumes of information on this subject? Very boring and tedious!

Nonetheless, it is very important for you to understand Medicare. Your choices will have an **enormous** impact on your finances, and where you can go for medical care for the remainder of your years!

Timing is *very important* with Medicare, so read on! You will quickly gain the necessary basic knowledge here. *No need to be stressed or confused!* Consider hiring a Medicare Advisor to guide you. Then you can get back to doing what you like to do, sooner!

After reading this guide, you have the

option of consulting with me about your personal Medicare questions, or special circumstances, and receiving my recommendations, for a flat fee.

See https://www.medicare-consultant.com

You will receive expert tips on analyzing plans, avoiding costly mistakes, and choosing an insurance company, all <u>before</u> your initial enrollment period, the most *critical* time to have this information! Having this information will not only save you money, now and in the future, but will affect the *quality* of health care you receive when you need it the most!

My Guide to Medicare takes you through the basic steps of signing up for Medicare, and understanding the important decisions you need to make after that is done, and having all of the information *before* you turn 65!

TERMINOLOGY OF MEDICARE

<u>AOE</u> – Annual Open Enrollment – October 15th through December 7th, each year, as of December 2017. You can change plans during this time, if you choose to, each year.

<u>CMS</u> – Centers for Medicare and Medicaid.

<u>Catastrophic Coverage</u> – Once you have spent $5,000 out-of-pocket on medications (it includes the requisite $3,750 as of 2018), you are out of the coverage gap (or donut hole). It assures you only pay a small coinsurance amount or co-payment for covered drugs, for the rest of the calendar year.

<u>Disenrollment Period</u> – January 1 – February 14, each year, as of December 2017. If you are enrolled in a Medicare Advantage Plan, you can leave the plan and switch back to

original Medicare. This period *cannot* be used to switch from one Medicare Advantage plan to another, one drug plan to another, or change from original Medicare to a Medicare Advantage plan.

<u>Donut Hole</u> – The donut hole is also called "the gap". As of 2018, once you *and* your plan have spent $3,750 on *covered* medications, you are in the *gap*. This amount can change each year. This gap is where you pay the *most* for your medications – *more about that later*. The next stage is called "catastrophic coverage".

<u>Dual Eligible</u> – Some people are eligible for both Medicare and Medicaid. If you have Medicare and full Medicaid, most of your health care costs will be covered.

<u>Formulary</u> - An official list which gives details of medicines that are covered

by your insurance company.

<u>IEP</u> – Initial Enrollment Period – a seven month period around your 65th birthday—the three months before your birth month, the month of your birthday, and the three months after your birth month.

<u>MA</u> – A Medicare Advantage Plan allows you to have "set" medical costs so you can plan and budget. *More details in Chapter 6.*

<u>MAPD</u> – A Medicare Advantage Plan with a prescription drug plan included.

<u>Medigap</u> – Plans that cover the *gaps* that original Medicare leaves you with. These are also commonly called Supplemental Plans (i.e., A, B, F, G…).

<u>Part A</u> – This is part of original Medicare from the Government, and there is no cost, if you have worked at

least 10 years in the U.S. and paid taxes, or a spouse paid taxes. In general, it covers some hospital expenses.

Part B – This is part of original Medicare from the Government, and *does* have a cost, which is based upon your income, and what CMS sets as the cost. In general, it covers some doctors' visits, x-rays, and lab work.

Part C – This is also known as a Medicare Advantage Plan. Some plans include prescription coverage (part D).

Part D – A prescription drug plan – a stand-alone plan.

SEP – Special Enrollment Period. There are many situations that are considered to be "life changing" events that allow you a SEP. Some examples include; moving to a new address that is not in your plan's service area, or you become eligible for low income assistance, or you move to an assisted living facility. Those are just a few examples, of many.

<u>SNF (Skilled Nursing Facility)</u> – Part A covers skilled nursing care in a Skilled Nursing Care Facility, for a limited time, and under certain conditions.

Keep in mind, there are many more terms, but these are the most common ones you should know, in order to help you understand Medicare.

Also, if you are looking for interesting and reliable information on health, diseases, statistics, and more, look at the Journal of the American Medical Association, online (reference on pg. 31).

[1] WHAT YOU NEED TO GET STARTED

Make a list of your doctors' names, *locations*, and telephone numbers. You will need this information to see what plans they accept. Think about whether or not you are "married" to your doctors, or if you would consider changing providers for a plan that better suits your health needs, and of course, your budget.

Make a list of the names of your medications, milligrams, dosages, and whether or not they are generic, if you know. You will need this information to estimate costs of medications, and choosing the right drug plan.

Your Medicare Consultant can, and should check all of the above information for you. Having the above will allow you to see what plans your doctors accept, and what medications are in the formulary for the insurance plans you are considering.

Decide what you can afford to pay per month, *in addition to Part B which is $134/month as of 2018*. If you have a higher income than $85,000, as a single tax payer, it will cost you more.

Regarding cutting Medicare benefits to seniors, as we often see in the news, this is from Wikipedia.org, and it explains the changes that took place in Medicare under the Whitehouse Administration of 2015:

> Retirement of the Baby Boom generation—which by 2030 is projected to increase enrollment to more than 80 million as the number of workers per enrollee declines from 3.7 to 2.4—and rising overall health care costs pose substantial financial challenges to the program. Medicare spending is projected to increase from $523 billion in 2010 to just over $1 trillion by 2022.[21] Baby-boomers' health is also an important factor: 20% have five or more chronic conditions, which will add to the future cost of health care

(www.cms.gov, 2012). **In response to these financial challenges, Congress made substantial cuts to future payouts to providers as part of PPACA in 2010 and the Medicare Access and CHIP Reauthorization Act of 2015 (MACRA)** and policymakers have offered a number of additional competing proposals to reduce Medicare costs further. *See* https://en.wikipedia.org/wiki/Medicare_(United States)

You can draw your own conclusions with the above information, as well as do further research, if interested.

[2] WHEN TO START PREPARING

Three months before your birthday is the best time to start. The IEP (initial enrollment period) is a *seven month* period around your 65th birthday.

As noted above, your IEP consists of the three months *before* your birth month, the *month of your birthday*, and the three months *after* your birth month. For example: My birthday is August 2. My IEP would be May, June, July, August, September, October, and November.

If you miss this Initial Enrollment Period, you may have to pay late enrollment penalties. Also, it's important to know -- you will miss your *one and only* chance to enroll in a Medigap plan, <u>*without*</u> *medical underwriting*, and/or without paying more than you would have. If you miss the IEP, and apply for a Medigap plan, you could be denied, based on health conditions. This is the case unless you qualify for a SEP. *Please re-read the above!*

If you are under age 65, and disabled, you can apply for Medicare. It usually takes two years to get that approval, once you have been designated as permanently disabled. It could be approved sooner in a situation of a critical illness, such as cancer. In that case, some insurance companies offer Medigap plans, and some do not. The ones that do, will charge a higher than normal premium, due to the disability, knowing that you will need more than the usual medical care.

Mark your calendar for three months before your 65th birthday. Recently, a friend of mine said he has been so busy, that he forgot to sign up for Medicare. He now has fewer options, and some possible penalties. Don't let that happen to you.

Timing is critical! Don't miss your Initial Enrollment Period, it can be costly!

[3] ELIGIBILITY FOR MEDICARE

In general, everyone who has worked at least 10 years in the United States, and paid taxes into Medicare, is entitled to sign up for Part A (hospitalization coverage), at age 65, with no cost. If you have worked less than 10 years (or 40 quarters), you can still get Part A, but there will be a cost, depending upon how many credits you have from your work.

In almost all cases, you will also want to sign up for Part B at the same time you sign up for Part A. *See more information on that in Chapters 5 and 6*. There is a cost to part B. It is based on your income, and government regulations.

Ideally, you will apply for Part A and B during the three months before your birthday month. Your Medicare card should arrive before your 65th birthday. *It will take effect on the 1st day of your birth month.* Using the example from above in Chapter 2, my birthday is August 2nd. That would mean *my* effective date of coverage would be August 1st of my 65th year.

[4] NEXT STEPS IN THE PROCESS

To sign up for Medicare Part A and Part B (assuming you will need part B because you don't receive the equivalent from your former employer), contact the government either by telephone, in person, or online.

First step: During your IEP you should call 1-(800)-Medicare (800-633-4227), or for the hearing impaired, (800) 486-2048. Or, visit your local social security office, or you can apply online at www.ssa.gov. They may ask you about enrolling in Part D (a drug plan), but hold off on that until you know if you will choose a Medigap Plan, or a MAPD.

Second step: Do your research by reading guides, such as this one. If you would like to read the official government guide, it is located here: www.medicare.gov. Be aware-- there are many websites that are *very similar*, *purposely* – and they are actually insurance companies. To avoid being pressured into buying a plan immediately, make sure you are looking at the ".gov" website, and not a .com, .net, .org, etc.

I would advise you <u>not</u> to put your telephone number out on the Internet while researching. You will likely receive close to a hundred phone calls! You will receive "tons" of mail about signing up for Medicare, even without going on the Internet.

Third step: Consider whether you should hire a professional Medicare Consultant. A good advisor can offer tips on saving money, educate you on important questions to ask your insurance agent, and make personalized recommendations. Those discussions will be based on your current health, county of residence, future travel plans, and financial needs. Some people qualify for additional financial assistance to pay for Part B, and Part D, through CMS (Centers for Medicare and Medicaid Services). After a consult, you will have a better understanding on whether you should shop for a Medigap Plan, or a Medicare Advantage Plan, and the reasons.

The fourth step: Actually look at *those* plans that are offered in your area.

Consider the history and reputation of the insurance companies offering the plans. Has the company previously left your state and then come back to your state to conduct business? Have you ever heard of the company? How are they rated on A.M. Best? You can Google www.ambest.com and see the financial rating of the company.

Compare benefits, including the network of providers, and of course, monthly premiums. This information is available online with various insurance companies that offer coverage in your state, on www.medicare.gov, and also through your chosen Medicare Consultant.

[5] WHAT DO PARTS, A, B, AND D OF ORIGINAL MEDICARE COVER?

Part A of original Medicare covers hospitalization if you meet the requirements of the "benefit period" (as specified on www.medicare.gov), which is at least a 3 day hospital stay, physician approved. You will pay a deductible of $1,340, as of 2018 for *each benefit period*. This means, for example, if you have two hospital stays for the calendar year, more than 60 days apart, you would pay that deductible twice. This is the case, unless you have a Medigap or Medicare Advantage plan that picks up those bills.

A more specific example of the above—let's say you go to the hospital on February 2, 2018, and stay there until February 10, 2018. You will be responsible for the $1,340 hospital deductible under Part A (again, unless you have a Medigap or Medicare Advantage plan that pays some, or all of the deductible). If you are then, admitted to the hospital *again* in June of 2018, you would owe another deductible of $1,340. Otherwise, Part A covers hospitalization as follows:

- Days 1–60: at a $0 cost for each benefit period ($0 in 2018)

- Days 61–90: you would pay $335 coinsurance per day of each benefit period (as of 2018)

- Days 91 and beyond: you pay $670 coinsurance per day for each "lifetime reserve day" after day 90, for each benefit period (you get up to 60 reserve days over your lifetime, as of 2018)

- Beyond lifetime reserve days, you pay all costs

Part B of original Medicare, covers doctors' visits, labs, x-rays, durable medical equipment (i.e. wheelchairs) outside of the hospital, and medications while in the hospital, etc.

Part B is an option –- meaning -- you don't have to buy it. The cost is based on your income and government regulation. However, I would always recommend you take Part B, unless you are retired from a company or entity that offers benefits *after* age 65. Common examples are; Railroad benefits, Federal benefits, Tricare, Union benefits, and school system benefits for retired teachers. These sometimes take the place of Part B. Speak to your benefits representative at your company before you retire. *Once again, the costs of Part B can change each year*.

Part A and Part B leave gaps in coverage; thus, *someone coined the term "medigap"*, which is also known as a "supplemental plan". Those gaps include things such as deductibles, co-payments, co-insurance, and other costs. This is where the *alphabet soup* comes in to play (i.e. Medigap plans A, B, F, G, K and others).

Some Medicare beneficiaries qualify for low income assistance with their payment for Part B, as well as Part D (prescription coverage). If this applies to you, there are several options your Medicare Consultant can explain, or you can just contact <u>www.medicaid.gov</u> for your State. Finding the right forms and telephone numbers can be complicated.

Part D covers prescription drugs. If you decide to buy a supplemental plan/medigap plan, you will also need to buy a prescription plan. Prices vary each year, and company to company. As of 2018, I have seen a range of approximately $35 to $75 a month for Part D.

Not signing up for Part D when you become eligible means you will likely pay a penalty, for the rest of your life. But, in some cases, it is to your advantage to delay signing up, and to pay a small penalty. For instance, if you do not take any medications and don't anticipate taking any for the year because you are very healthy, it may be the right decision to delay. Calculate the penalty by multiplying the "national base beneficiary premium" times 1%, times the full number of uncovered months. Let's say, as an example, you did not have Part D coverage for the first 10 months when you first became eligible--you would then calculate:

$35.02 (in 2018) x 1% x 10 months = $3.50. When you do sign up for Part D, add the $3.50 to each month's premium (for the rest of your life).

Your Medicare Consultant can help you estimate your drug costs, in order to help you assess when to sign up for Part D, and what plans may work the best for your situation.

It's important to know that if you are in the hospital, you would still have drug coverage, covered by Part B.

Once you are out of the hospital, Part D (or your MAPD) pays for medications as outlined in the Plan you chose.

What about coverage when traveling to a foreign country? Generally speaking, Medicare does *not* cover you while in a foreign country. However, *some* Medicare Advantage plans do, and *most* supplemental plans do, for emergencies.

Now, that you have digested the above information, let's review the pros and cons of Supplemental Plans as compared to Medicare Advantage Plans.

[6] SUPPLEMENTAL PLANS V. MEDICARE ADVANTAGE PLANS

In most states, there are many different companies that offer supplemental plans, as well as Medicare Advantage Plans. Just remember, you can only choose one type for each year, during annual open enrollment.

The biggest benefit to signing up for a supplemental plan (Medigap plan), **at age 65**, is that you do *not* have to answer medical questions.

If you wait until *after* the age of 65 (past

your IEP), you will have to answer medical questions, and _could be denied_, based upon health conditions. This is important to keep in mind, particularly if you have several medical issues, or are anticipating more medical care due to a health condition, or multiple conditions. The network of providers on most supplemental plans is _almost_ unlimited – this is one of the major benefits compared to a Medicare Advantage Plan.

If you decide to buy a Medicare Advantage Plan, consider that some of these come with a drug plan (referred to as a MAPD). These are _very cost effective_ plans, and work well on a tight budget. The only catch is to make sure you are happy with the network (hospitals, doctors, etc.), and that it covers your county of residence. The network of providers can change each year.

Also, a particular provider may have several offices, and _some locations may accept your plan as in network, while others may not. You must have both Part A and Part B of_ *original Medicare, in order to sign up for a Medicare Advantage Plan.*

In general, coverage is based on these items:

(1) federal and state laws (2) national coverage decisions made by CMS (the Centers for Medicare and Medicaid Services), and (3) local coverage decisions made by companies that process Medicare claims in your state.

For any type of plan above, the formulary can change each year. For more information on these types of plans, please visit my website at <u>www.medicare-consultant.com</u> or <u>www.medicare.gov</u>.

Also, as of now, each State has free advisors (volunteers) on Medicare at:

https://www.shiptacenter.org/

CONCLUSION

As you can see from this short guide on Medicare, it can be very complicated and confusing, and there is much information to know! It changes a bit each year. And, it can be over-whelming, to say the least!

Just as you would consult with a tax professional to do your taxes, or consult with an attorney on a legal matter, consider the value you will receive by consulting with a Medicare specialist. It will pay off for you in *many* ways!

Disclaimer: The author does not represent, nor claim to represent herself as part of any government program, entity, or office.

REFERENCES

www.medicare.gov, U.S. Government

www.opm.gov (for Federal Employees)

www.ssa.gov (Social Security Administration)

www.va.gov (for Veterans)

www.rrb.gov (for Railroad employees or retirees)

www.kff.org, Kaiser Family Foundation

seniorsresourceguide.com (free Medicare advice)

www.jamanetwork.com, Journal of the American Medical Association

ABOUT THE AUTHOR

Denise is highly skilled at analyzing insurance plans, explaining government regulations, and has written this easy to understand book – **My Guide to Medicare**. *It quickly sums up and explains what you need to do, and when. She earned her M.B.A. at the University of St. Thomas, in Houston, Texas, and makes her home in Florida. She is also a Licensed Insurance Agent in Florida.*